AF471358

ACTOR'S BLUEPRINT

by

RALPH KINNARD

Actor's Blueprint® is a trademark owned by the author.
The author's Web Site: http://www.miamiactingstudio.com

SECOND EDITION

ISBN 978-1105-555-442

If you can dream it,

you can do it.

Special thanks to Claude Carranza for re-editing, revising, translation and adding material and to Monica for the inspiration, I wouldn't be doing this without you !

FOREWORD

Nothing in the world compares to the excitement of creative work. There is a thrilling expectation the night before the start of filming a new movie, or preparing a new theatre play. The day of the premiere, rehearsal hours just fly by and “life makes sense”.

You feel incredibly alive and you don't have the slightest doubt that all the effort and the stressful months of rehearsals were worth it. Everything falls into place..

I started this journey on a fine summer day many years ago in Munich’s main square, called “Marienplatz”. I painted my face white and started performing street theatre. I was sixteen at the time, thrilled, scared, excited and without a clue as to what to do.

One hour passed without a single person stopping to watch me. I hadn't earned a single Deutsche Mark and only a stray dog was watching my “show”. I began to understand then and there that I needed to study and train seriously before I could really have something to offer to an audience.

My first stop was to study pantomime and theatre techniques based on the teachings of Etienne Decroux and Marcel Marceau in Germany. I learned to dissociate my head and neck movements, to rotate my elbows while keeping my hands and shoulders totally motionless and was then sent to the local ballet school to learn about postures. Needless to say, I was the ONLY boy in the group, which sounds promising, but as a skinny, tall German fellow in tights, well…, you get the picture.

At 21 I had the privilege to attend Philippe Gaulier's clowns academy in London. It was one of the most difficult things I ever intended: How do you make a group of 34 fellow clowns laugh?

We had special tasks to help us like: “Pretend you are a 1950 Peugeot washing machine” or “just pretend there is a nail in the wall and hang your jacket.”
The next and most important step happened in New York, where I finally got introduced to the “spoken work”.

I met great actors and teachers at the Lee Strasberg Theater Institute and at the Actor's Studio, who managed to eliminate my misconceptions about theatre, helped me eliminate my over-acting and showed me that good acting is not easy and lives in the simplicity of being.

There is something unique about the study of acting. Your own body and mind are the very instruments you will use. They are all you need to improvise, interact with other students and imagine yourself in a vast array of places and circumstances.

What should you expect from acting lessons? The classroom has to be a special place where you can explore your own personality in all possible situations. The teaching has to be first and foremost practical, and the student will have to act and improvise from the very beginning. There has to be absolute respect for the physical and emotional safety of everyone.

It also has to be a fun and entertaining experience. After all, we will not be performing open-heart surgery, nor will we be fixing a jet engine. We will be instilling art and creativity in our lives and this can only be joyful and pleasant.

Acting implies exploring and enlarging your life's experience, stretching your imagination and refining your sensibility. The enrichment it will bring shall remain yours forever.

I want to invite you to this special journey and this unique adventure and to help understand more about the craft, and what not to do.

THE ACTOR'S CRAFT

Konstantin Stanislavsky established the foundation of modern theatre acting, drawing the guidelines that every actor has to follow in order to develop natural behavior on stage in the book "An actor prepares".

Lee Strasberg had the opportunity to see a performance of Stanislavsky's Moscow Art Theatre to the United States in 1923. This experience of seeing first hand a group of actors without ego's at play had a profound impact on his life, leading the way to the creation of the Group Theater in New York in 1931, the Actor's Studio and the Lee Strasberg Theater Institute. He developed, refined and put into practice the "method" a technique that provides the actor with the means of reaching to his own talent "at any time, instantly".

This new approach to acting changed the movie industry. Actors like Marlon Brando, Rod Steiger, Dustin Hoffman, Gene Hackman, Robert de Niro, Paul Newman, Marilyn Monroe. Al Pacino, Harvey Keitel, to only name a few, set the standard for what is expected of an actor.

The greatest mystery and difficulty in art is INSPIRATION.

Without a technique that helps to put CONSISTENCY into our performances, the use of real emotions to impact the audience through what is know as emotional transference depends on luck! This great discovery separates the amateur from the professional. If you are not able to produce good casting and a good “act” at any given time – you will simply not find work.

And there is the difficulty: will your acting compare with a really good performance, without considering that you might be new at this or have not trained for years.

There have been important changes and improvements in communication since Strasberg's death on February 17th, 1982.

If we compare for instance an older movie like "The Graduate" with the more recent "Inglorious Bastards" we can easily perceive a substantial change in the actors performances. In much the same way we can compare the "The Cosby Show" with "Friends" or "Seinfeld" and notice big differences not only about the content of the TV series but also about the different rhythm of the scenes.

To help us understand these changes we have to first acknowledge that today's audiences are able to absorb and process information much faster than they did 20 years ago. The actor has had to adapt to these new developments.

We are living in an era of global, high-speed Communication. CNN, MTV and Internet permanently impact our minds and train us to immediately select the information we consider most important.

The pace of music videos has sped up, the images just flash in front of our eyes, but we still manage to capture their content. Technomusic could have existed 50 years ago our brains were but simply not ready to enjoy it. We needed to adapt and thus we have had to evolve, literally.

What is the PURPOSE of acting?

Acting involves an "act of creation" by which we provide our audience with the opportunity of having emotional experiences people can't have or feel in everyday life. That is the reason why Theater was invented 3.000 years ago in Greece and there is still the same need for emotional house-cleaning now as it was back then.

Action movies for instance raise our adrenaline levels and make us leave the movie theater highly motivated or even exhausted. Dramas help us release emotions, cry and allow us leave our personal sadness behind.

What are the necessary elements?

Every actor is always part of a particular society and draws his vital experience from it. Therefore, if his acting is based on his PERSONAL vision of the world, he’ll always connect to the reality of his audience.

However, an actor also has to understand "why" he is different from ANY OTHER ACTOR and project it to the public through drama, through acting. Let's always remember that the unique personal way that every individual has of looking at life is unique, special and therefore interesting.

Many actors make the big mistake of trying to imitate another actor or reproduce exactly how other people act.

Please do pick up a piece of paper and drop it to the floor.

Now repeat this exercise.

What is the surprising outcome?

It will never land at the same precise place on the floor.

An actor, by definition a much more complicated being than a piece of paper, would never feel exactly the same at two different moments in time; as his emotional inner energy changes second by second simply HE IS NOT THE SAME PERSON he was five seconds ago.
Therefore he will not be able to even imitate himself exactly as he has already changed.

Therefore to try to imitate what another actor is doing is useless.

RELAXATION AND SENSE MEMORY

The actor's instruments are his own body, emotions and ideas. It naturally follows that he needs to be in command of these "tools" when entering his workplace, be it the theatre stage, movie or TV studio.

Some time ago we had an actress in our classroom who was about to act an important role in a TV soap opera. Her own anxiety, coupled with the TV station's relentless pressure and demands, made her forget an essential part of the acting work: ART.

I asked her the following crucial questions:

- How can you act naturally and perform well Monday morning at 7.00 am?

- Where do you draw your inspiration from Wednesday night at 11.00 pm when you are exhausted and there are still a dozen scenes left to be filmed?

- How can you possibly manage to act if you had a big fight at home the night before and you are still tense, maybe even hurting?

The actor uses his emotions in much the same way a car uses gasoline.

Your emotional balance is the AMOUNT of fuel you have to TELL A STORY. It doesn't matter "what" you feel. A story can be told a millon different ways. All that matters is that the story is TOLD. (just like the example of the falling paper that ALWAYS ends up on the floor, the actor always needs to USE the same lines and finish at the END of the script).

RELAXATION

Here is an example of a normal relaxation technique to "LEVEL" your emotions and read the FUEL-METER on how you feel:

1. Sit down in a comfortable position: Put your feet flat on the floor, let your arms hang down and close your eyes.

2. Release the tension of your facial muscles, mouth, jaws, eyebrows, ...

3. Relax your eyes, look inside yourself and feel the "weight" of your brain.

4. Then relax from the top down: first the neck, then the shoulders, arms, forearms, hands; next the spine, belly, pelvis, buttocks, legs.

5. Take a deep, slow breath and "point" it in the direction of your heart. Then mentally "breath out your stress" slowly, making a slightly whistling noise. Repeat it a few times, listening to your respiration.

6. Finally take a very deep breath in to finish the exercise, and slowly open your eyes.

This relaxation can be performed at home while listening to some soothing music you particularly like. It can take you five to 10 minutes, but you can master it and accomplish a quick relaxation in as little time as one minute, even 30 seconds.

You will be surprised to know how many actors and actresses obtain a great benefit from this fast relaxation, thus leveling their emotional and physical state in order to enhance their acting performance.

Of course, we are not defining or using our emotions yet. On the contrary, we are draining them out and relaxing our body.

(It's important to note, that the emotions we repress tend to remain "trapped" in our body and become the causes of psychosomatic illnesses such as skin, digestive, problems, insomnia etc.)

SENSE MEMORY

Constantin Stanislavsky went to see a theatre play in Moscow in the 1890s. He enjoyed the plot and was especially ecstatic about the performance of the starring actress. A few days later he invited one of his best friends to see the play so they could both admire the acting virtuosity of the leading lady.

They both were quickly disappointed: the same actress who had given such a raving performance a few days earlier was now over-acting, moving around the scene with no realism, and saying her lines in a rather mechanical uninspiring way. Constantin's friend was annoyed and decided to leave after the first act, but Stanislavsky, very frustrated, decided not to leave and keep watching, wondering what on earth could have happened.

In the middle of the second act there was a little accident; nothing special, really, just something that can happen during a theatre performance ... The actress tripped against a piece of furniture and almost fell to the floor, but managed to recover.

It was then that something really extraordinary

happened: She suddenly started to act differently, very much in the way she did the first time Stanislavsky attended the play, and she maintained her newly recovered brilliancy until the end of the third act.

Sense memory is the cable that connects and plugs the actor in with his talent at will.

What does this mean?

Let's begin with an example that can be familiar to all of us: We often have improvs at the Studio where a couple has a big argument while they are in a car. Two chairs are put together and the students are invited to "get into the car and have a big fight" while they are driving to, say, have dinner at a restaurant.

Typically, the guy will "open" the left door of the car mimicking a quick turn of the key, then will sit on his chair and will eventually –not always- mimic again a turn of the key to start the engine while she sits on the other chair without even bothering to feign opening the passenger's door. (Let's not be sexist here: she can be the driver, and the passenger guy will often forget to “open” the passenger’s door)

Later, the student driving the car will probably look sideways to his “wife” for 5 or 10 seconds solid, ceasing to care about the road where he is supposed to be driving. In some cases they will completely let go of the wheel and gesticulate while having this big argument with their passenger partner.

Careless beginners … Aren’t they?

But then we can also attend a theatre play and notice that one of the characters drinks whiskey as if it were Nestea (which is probably what his glass contains). Another character will hold what is supposed to be a diamond bracelet as if it is the piece of junk it certainly is, then will open a letter sent by the President of the United States in exactly the same way you treat junk mail.

Sense Memory is a tool that can solve these problems and make the scenes look truthful and authentic.

When we open the door of our car we hold and turn the key in a particular way. Maybe We put the other hand on the roof of the vehicle and we have our own particular way of opening the door. Also, we will do most of the talking while we are NOT looking at our passenger.

If we use our “brain memory” to recreate this, we’ll turn into bad copycat actors. Our logical brain is NOT creative and cannot answer to NEW events. It can only TAPE events and store information.

You have two kinds of memory:

Our mental “brain” memory, and our Sense memory.

If you start acting based on just your mind memory you may end up imitating some actor you have seen in a movie and not even be aware that you are doing it. Of course great actors produce great acting, like Jack Nicholson, but it is impossible for another actor to repeat any of his performances. The reason is simple:

He is somebody else.

On the other hand, if you establish a connection with your own emotions based on your own experiences, your life becomes the raw material of your art.

It naturally ensues that each individual has to find his/her own style and that is where the practice of

SENSE MEMORY becomes essential. Your body cells have in storage all the information of your life, like a "file" or hard-disk drive. If you succeed in connecting with that information, be it your first kiss, a special rainy night, or an unforgettable day at the beach, your acting will become interesting, lively, and specific to you only.

This SENSE MEMORY connection will produce unexpected and unpredictable acting choices. You might for example get connected with an exciting flirt you had last summer by the seaside, but that day you were being also bitten by mosquitoes and got sun-struck. We will be able to watch yourself telling silly jokes and looking intensely at your partner while also feeling that your body is slightly annoyed by the sunburn and inconvenienced by the mosquitoes, thus having a realistic and authentic experience based on your uniqueness as a person.

You will be asked to perform SENSE MEMORY exercises in order to find the "cable" that will allow you to connect with the "hard-disk" of your own subconscious world and empower your acting with these new tools.

TRY OUT EXERCISE:

What is your first drink in the morning? We will assume it is a cup of coffee. OK? The very next time you have it you must take 10 minutes to work on the way you drink your coffee. Examine the cup carefully, touch it, check the weight, take a sip of the liquid slowly, feel its temperature and taste, then swallow it. Repeat it two or three times, then put the cup aside.

Now, for another 10 minutes, explore the cup in an imaginary way doing the same physical actions. Observe. Feel the weight and the warmth of the cup. Hold it like you held the real one.

Attention! This has to be exploring, not mimicking.

It is as if you are asking your eyes if they can remember the exact look of the cup, asking your hand if it is able to remember its weight and temperature, your nostrils if they can do the same with the smell the coffee, then asking your mouth if it can "experience" the taste … even if you can hear the noise you make while drinking it.

The answer you get can be a "yes" or a "no" if you don't feel anything.

Do not worry if you don't feel anything; the point now is to get concentrated on the exercise. (Please don't think about what you plan to do tonight, don't remember your boyfriend/girlfriend, and don't think about food either; not even about money!)

We mentioned the sight and the touch. Let's move now to smell. Was the coffee you had earlier strong? Did it have sugar and milk?

You may at some point feel bored by this exercise and begin to wonder if it is worth the effort. Do not allow your mind to play games with you! We have to concentrate on the senses, and this is an essential exercise to train you.

Let's move on to another sense: taste. Take the first sip. Is it a hot? Rather cold? Does it have enough sugar? The coffee usually spreads inside your mouth, slips under your tongue, makes contact with your teeth. Swallow, please. Did you drink all the coffee you had in your mouth? Did you have to swallow twice?

Go ahead and have another sip.

Don't worry or agonize if you don't feel any of these things.

After all, the cup of hot coffee is not really there.

Again, the important thing is to concentrate.

Use any trick that can be helpful for you … Imagine for instance that Steve Spielberg is paying you $10.000 to film you doing this exercise.

(Don't think about Spielberg's money if the ten thousand are distracting you from the cup of coffee)

There are a number of exercises that you will be adding to this one: shaving in front of your mirror, taking a shower, putting on your make up, etc.

It is very very important that you do this every day, alone, at home; not only at the Miami Acting Studio.

If you want to see sessions from the Miami Acting Studio check out www.miamiactingstudioblog.com so you can see it for yourself.

Your concentration will be developing constantly and you will have a clear, conscious and permanent way of directly reaching your subconscious personal talent.

SENSE MEMORY will make you act in a realistic and specific way. For instance, your behavior in a church will be very different from the way you would act at the beach, or having lunch at McDonalds. You will be creating a tridimensional, real and authentic character.

An actor who was about to start filming his first motion picture asked the following question: "I have to act like a drug addict, but I don't have any experience with drugs. How can I make it personal, specific and real?"

Answer: Use SENSE MEMORY about some alcoholic beverage, and then mix it with some exercise concerning heat. This might cause a strong physical reaction very close to what is feels like to be on drugs.

There are hundreds of exercises (fantasy objects, animals, places, etc., to name but a few) that you can use to cover about any conceivable need you may have as an actor.

It is now time to start rehearsing your scene.

STEP I : COMMUNICATING WITH YOUR PARTNER

We can only see about one tenth of an iceberg; the other nine tenths are hidden under the water.

In every scene you will have a sub-text that is "hiding". It consists of the pre-existing relationship between the characters and the objectives they have in the scene. This goes much further than the first impression you get from the text the first time you read it.

Let's take an example: In the movie THE GODFATHER II there is a scene where Vito Corleone (Robert de Niro) is driving a car carrying stolen goods. Panucci (Gaston Moschin) hops into the car uninvited and explains to Vito that he has to pay protection money to him. Vito politely answers that he may be willing to contribute after he checks with his two business associates. Panucci helps himself to some clothes in Vito´s inventory, agrees to have a meeting in order to receive Vito´s money, and leaves the car. The dialog is short, humorous, and businesslike. But the crucial information that colors everything - information that we spectators have, but the character Panucci does not - is our knowledge that Panucci had Vito fired from his job one year earlier in order to have his own nephew to take Vito's place as store helper. Panucci didn't notice who was fired then, but Vito recognizes Panucci at once and remembers he was put in a very difficult economic position at a time when his son was seriously sick.

We don't pay too much attention to the actual talk during the scene. What catches our attention is Vito´s permanent sweet smile while he evaluates Panucci and agrees with everything he says. I would dare say that the more Vito (Robert de Niro) smiles, the better we understand that he is going to give Panucci a tough time. The sub-text is much more important than the dialogue.
It is also very important to watch different versions of the same play, say Hamlet, and compare the movie acted and directed by Laurence Olivier to the one directed by Franco Zefirelli with Mel Gibson, and also to the one produced by Kenneth Brannagh placing Hamlet in the 19th century. Not a word of the text has been changed, but the three movies are completely different.

As we indicated in the beginning of this chapter, if you memorize your text quickly and decide how you have to ¨feel¨ and ¨act¨ it, you are already in trouble. To make matters worse, are you paying any attention to your partner?

There is a proverb that goes ¨If you have lemons, make lemonade. If you have oranges, don't make lemonade, make orange juice¨.

You will have to react in a different way to each actor you have in front of you.

What is the proper way then of learning your lines?

- First, you have to manage to "own" your text without any pre-established way of saying it

- You also have to create a relationship with your partner(s) that is credible, based on the way each actor perceives life

Please consider this line of dialogue:

¨Listen, John. This is the last time I will let you borrow my car. You are so disrespectful. How could you let your dog stay in my car? The whole place stinks like a dog. Next time I see your pet I'm going to kill it¨

Obvious ... Isn't it?

No.

Not at all.

You are going to realize it in about one minute:

-Say this text with a big smile on your face ...

-Then, say it laughing out loud ...

-Now, say it looking ashamed and embarrassed to say it ...

-Next, say it yelling out loud ...

-Then, say it with indifference, coldness ...

Yes. As you now see, there is not a way better than other. We will probably even feel that acting it with anger is the least interesting one!

Also, the attitude of your partner in the scene will probably trigger different reactions from you, and you will now feel free to show indifference, sarcasm, etc., during the dialogue

Now concentrate on the other actor, your partner in the scene:

YOUR RELATIONSHIP WITH YOUR PARTNER IS THE KEY TO YOUR ACTING.

If each actor is in a “different world” the public will

quickly detect that they are watching two “autistic characters” ignoring each other. Communication and inter-acting are the very material great scenes are made of.

You have to know your partner, to him/her, to understand his/her vision of the scene and the way your partner perceives the existing relationship between the characters. We will use the following technique in order to develop this knowledge about your partner and create a personal relationship between you:

Explain to him/her the scene you are going to act, as if your partner knew absolutely nothing about it. Do speak in the first person (as if you were your own character) and do not show any emotion at this point.

We will use a scene from the movie ¨A MI ME GUSTA¨ with Monica Pasqualotto and Jonathan Ashford:
(www.amimegustapelicula.net)

Margarita/Paul

M - What are you doing here?

P - Why didn't you go to work today?

M - You came to ask me that?

P - Could you lend me a towel, please?

(Margarita goes inside the house while Paul waits outside doing breathing exercises. She comes back bringing a roll of toilet paper, gives it to Paul; he dries his forehead with it then takes a piece of paper from his pocket and reads it to Margarita)

¨Margarita, let me explain: All my life I have wanted an orange. It was the most exotic fruit there was. I understand it, I know how it tastes, and I know how it can be used in the kitchen. But now I know mango, and the sweet taste of mango. Everything changed for me, and now I feel like a fruit salad¨

... So much so that I even called Doctor Brian, my shrink back in London, because I broke up with Inga and I wanted to tell you about that ... And he told me I have to go through process so I am not unaware and not do anything hastily, and fate can be accomplished. Do you understand?

M - Anything else?

P - No. This is for you.

(He gives her an envelope and leaves)

(Margarita's mother arrives and reads the letter in

the envelope, then yells to everyone that Margarita has her letter of recommendation.)

You could now explain the scene to your partner in more or less this way: "Well, I am Paul, a famous chef; I have written several best selling cuisine books. I am English and went to Venezuela to teach cooking to the team of the restaurant of a 5 star hotel in Caracas. Margarita was one of the cooks of the team.

I first hated her, but then we made a bet and she cooked a great meal for me at her parent's house. They invited me to go to the beach and there I fell in love with Margarita.

Back at the hotel, just when I was in the middle of this fantastic romance with her, I found my English fiancée Inga was at the hotel in Caracas.
I couldn't react properly and just interrupted my romance with Margarita, instead of telling Inga I didn't love her anymore. But now I have taken the decision to leave Inga, and stay in Venezuela with Margarita. She didn't come to work and I went to her house."

Once you do this, the actress can talk to you in the same informative way, as if you didn't know anything about the scene.

"I am Margarita. I was the chef at the Caracas hotel, but left for England. I enormously admired Paul and came close to having his autograph on my copy of his last book. His fiancée Inga fired me from my job in the London restaurant where I was working and I had to leave England. Back in Caracas I had to take the lowest position in the hotel restaurant. I was asked to pick up Paul at the airport and bring him to Caracas; he hates me because I was late and I drove in the usual careless crazy way Venezuelans do. I started a cold guerrilla war in the kitchen against Paul, because he is very pretentious and thinks we don't know anything about cooking. I finally made a bet: I will prepare a meal for him at my parent's house and quit my position at the restaurant if he doesn't like the food. He loves the food and agrees to be invited to our house on the beach. We fall in love.

Back at the hotel there is the English rattlesnake who fired me in London, and I have to hear she is Paul's fiancée. He freezes and practically ignores me.

The next day I didn't go back to work, I am home with my sister, telling her how much I hate Paul when the door bell rings and there he is at the door, all wet from the rain".

NEXT STEP: IT IS NOT ACTING TIME YET.

Sit down facing your partner, put your feet flat on the floor and take the script for the scene. Read your first line without saying anything. Memorize it if you can.

Now, look your partner in the eyes and say the line while you smile lightly. Do not act it, pronounce the sentences flatly, in a neutral voice. It doesn't matter at all if you need to go back to read your script because you don't remember all of it. Just go back and reread your line silently, but then make sure that you pronounce every word while looking at your partner's eyes and that he/she is looking at you.

When it is the other actor's turn, he/she will say his/her line in exactly the same way with a flat, neutral tone of voice. Smile a little when speaking. Pronounce words only when both actors are looking in each other's eyes.

If there is a long line, just break it down into a number of pieces and do not hurry the process.

This exercise can be repeated two or three times.

Its purpose is to listen to yourself and your partner while observing what reactions the text triggers in you both.

Again, remember that it is crucial that the text is spoken coldly, without expression, with no trace of acting. You need to stay open to any and all possibilities, by PRECISELY NOT CHOOSING ANY, just yet.

STEP II : THE LOGIC OF THE SCENE

What do you want? Who are you? Where are you?

Now, you have to ask yourself this: What do I want to accomplish in this scene? What is my character's goal?

Here are a few examples:

- "I want to kill her/him"
- "I want to make love to her/him"
- "I want to sell my car "

If your goal requires a long explanation, or if what you want to accomplish is not clear in your mind, YOU SIMPLY WON'T BE ABLE TO ACT IT PROPERLY.

Here is very good example: "Well, I might be interested in talking to her, of course, if she can ... about a minute, more or less, maybe ... and I believe she should think this is OK, if ... "

This is not a goal. This is a very long explanation that shows that you don´t know what you want to accomplish.
Do not complicate things: Your goal is what you want, clear and simple; and it should take just a few words to be described. Example: "I need to tell her that I love her"

Of course, you need to keep in mind that this is not decided by the actor because the playwright shows you what you have to do.

In order to enlarge your knowledge of the character you have to ask yourself the following questions, as if you really were the character:

- What are my first and last name?

- What are my parent's first names?

- When is my birthday? My zodiac sign? (The Chinese zodiac year is fine too.)

- How old am I?

- Do I have brothers, sisters? What are their names and professions?

- How good is my relationship with my family?

- Where was I born in?

- Where do I live now? What is my house like? What is my room like?

- Where do I work?

- Who was my best friend when I was little?

- Who is my best friend now?

- What do we do when we are together?

- Do I have a girlfriend/boyfriend? Am I married? What is her/his name? (Do I have a wife/husband + a lover too?)

- What is my worst fear? Can I trace its origin?

- What is my favorite food?

- Do I smoke? Drink? ... Any bad habits?

- What are my favorite pastimes?

- What were my best holidays?

- What car would I like to have? Do I have a car? (Just in case: is the car I have the one I want to have?)

- What is my worst guilt?

- What was my life's greatest loss?

- Who am I? ... (Tough question?)

- Where do I come from?

- What is the funniest thing about this scene?

- What happened in the last scene where I appeared, just before this one?

- What happened five minutes before I entered the scene I am acting in now?

- What are the obstacles I have to overcome?

- What do I need to do to fight these obstacles successfully?

- Do I have sense of humor?

- What do I want to do in this particular scene? We absolutely need a verb here: TELL her, KILL him, STEAL the money, etc.

- What is my input in the play?

This list will be an excellent guideline to deepen your knowledge of the character. Now, it is very likely that many of the answers do not appear in the script, but this is not a problem at all : JUST MAKE THEM UP. You have to create a real person, with secrets, wishes and dreams of his own. Also, the very fact that you answer a number of questions making the answers up does get you more inside the character.

Next, you need to ask yourself questions about the place where the scene is supposed to take place:

- What time is it?

- What is the weather like?

- How does the place smell?

-What can you see in the place?

Always bear in mind that the place is crucial to your acting.
You may have to be in a McDonald's restaurant, or in the White House or even in a goat market in Morocco.

Of course, you will have to say your lines very differently in each of these places. The first pitfall will obviously be to try an intellectual approach to the place, like pinching your nose and using a newspaper to fan your face in order to make us believe you are in a goat market in Morocco, but it will be common place and fake.

Instead, sense memory will come to your help here.

WE ARE NOW AT A CRUCIAL CROSSROADS.

You have all the necessary information about your character and the place where the scene is supposed to happen. What now?

1. If you have a lot in common with the character, and the action takes place in a living room similar to the one you have in your house, don’t look for anything else. There is no need for technique here. As the saying goes: "If it is not broken, don’t try to fix it"

2. If you have important differences with the character, and are not familiar with, say, a goat market in Morocco, you will need to use the SUBSTITUTION TECHNIQUE.

Let’s begin with the different traits of your character and yourself. Please take a sheet of paper and explore your differences by first writing them down:

NAME OF THE CHARACTER

Wants… from life

Hates ...

Loves ...

Needs …right now

Has just lived ...

Feels that ...

Is confused by ...

Is angry about ...

Is sad because ...

Is happy about ...

Where is he? ...

Now put YOUR OWN NAME and write about your life right now
(PERSONAL AND SPECIFIC!)

Wants …from life

Hates ...

Loves ...

Needs… right now

Has just lived ...

Feels that ...

Is confused by ...

Is angry about ...

Is sad because ...

Is happy about ...

Where is he? ...

EXAMPLE from the movie "A MI ME GUSTA"

I don't mix up love with phrases about "fruit salad", but I remember how nervous I was telling my wife, that I was in love with her.

I don't plan on change my life right now, but I can clearly identify with not wanting to live in my home country of Germany.

As you can see, as a first resource, I substitute the character troubles by troubles of my own that have the same emotional strength.

It is also essential that you manage to love, or at least be sympathetic to an unpleasant, even despicable character you have to play. If I completely reject him, I simply can't act him well. This can be very hard on you sometimes, and you have to overcome it.

My personal experience was very stressful and traumatic when I had to play the part of the rapist in EXTREMITIES. During my first rehearsal I was absolutely unable to act the part, and started to cry because I felt sympathetic to the poor actress playing the part of the raped girl. My teacher Elizabeth Kemp had me use my personal fears and nightmares until I could reach the necessary degree of brutality and violence.

Let's mention here that Marlon Brando was known and highly admired for his ability to use animals as the basis for his SENSE MEMORY EXERCICES.

During his first meeting with director Francis Ford Coppola, Brando stated, "this Godfather is a bulldog". And if you take the trouble of watching some scenes from the movie "THE GODFATHER" again you will readily perceive this strong, potentially dangerous, family guard dog lying beneath the features and make up of Brando's Godfather.

Let's take it one step further. Suppose you have to play a very neurotic character. In order to create an interesting physical behavior we can use one very special feature of SENSE MEMORY: the "fantasy object".

This object is something that is quite real for you and triggers a very specific physical reaction in your body. For instance, let's imagine three mosquitoes flying constantly around your head. Only you are able to see them.

If you practice this "3 mosquitoes around my head" SENSE MEMORY exercise then you may add it to your rehearsals little by little. You will observe if this new physical behavior fulfills the Director's requirements; if it does, you did great.

This particular application is also known as "The Theatre of the Mind". The spectators are not going to know about the exercise that you are performing. They will just watch your performance and see that you stay 100% within the logic of the scene. Nobody can read your mind, nor research the way you got ready for the scene.

As an artist, you must never share this information with your audience.

In very much the same way, we can apply the Theatre of the Mind to the place where you are supposed to be. If the script says that you are at the White House in Washington, you can work on the "private situation" of being naked in front of others. In order to act like you are in the presence of the President you may just imagine that you are naked: this will dictate a physical position of little mobility, noticeable rigidity, with your hands carefully crossed in front of you ... A most respectful and deferential attitude to the President, indeed.

The number of combinations like these is practically unlimited and will make us able to solve any acting difficulty.

This is a very simplistic approach to Sense Memory and you need to put in long hours to actually make it work – the important thing is to give you an idea of what kind of tools are available.

There is a limitless number of ways you can use SENSE MEMORY to help you enhance your performance. You can choose a person you know who might have some of the traits of the character you are trying to perfect. You can observe and study him/her carefully, in order to "substitute" that person with yourself.

If you have trouble establishing a relationship with your partner during a love scene, you may "substitute" the place where you are with another have by another one that brings you back romantic memories. You can also add some sense memory of a nice alcoholic drink. Then, if you "substitute" that actress with your real life sweetheart, you can be assured your acting will be excellent.

On the contrary, if you have to play the part of a drug addict having a crisis, you can again substitute the place of the scene in your mind with a very humid and hot beach that you are familiar with, and add the fantasy of a cockroach climbing up your motionless right leg ...

These two elements of sense memory ("whole body element" and "unpleasant fantasy object") will certainly produce a very perturbed looking behavior in you.

Now, let's not forget that your relationship with your partner comes first during the scene. This means that you are not to practice these exercises while you are acting. You have to practice tirelessly and have them ready ... You will then need some sensation, like touching an imaginary ammonia bottle, that will start your sense memory during the scene.

When the CIA first used lie detectors, suspects quickly found that they could fool the machine by putting nails in their shoes and hurting themselves on command. We actors can accomplish the same goal without hurting themselves ... through SENSE MEMORY.

Let's finish this section with two interesting stories about actors:

Dustin Hoffman once went to the set after a sleepless night and a hangover in order to be ready to give more reality to a scene. The director asked him to go home, get a good rest, and trust his great talent instead.

STEP III - IMPROVISATIONS

By now, you already have an accurate idea about what you have to do in your scene, but NO, do not learn your lines YET.

You need to do improvisations "around" your scene, scenes that are not in the movie, but are essential in the LIFE of the character.

"Improvs", as they are called, will put your ideas to the test and will always improve your relationship with your partner
(good acting will always seem like an Improvisation).

During the scene, we spectators want to watch a character 100% involved in the action who doesn't know what the outcome of the scene is and who tries his very best to overcome the obstacles he is facing.

All time you invest in getting ready for the scene will inevitably improve your final performance.

This process can quite properly be compared to the growth of a plant or a flower: Let it develop, let it mature; never try to stretch it because it will break. We have to acknowledge that the creation process has its own rhythm that has to be duly respected.

There are a few strict rules applying to improvisations:

- Don’t throw any object

- Do not touch your partners unless it is previously discussed and agreed. Example: "You can touch my hands, face and feet". You need your partner’s trust and consideration, and vice versa. Also, a good actor can work wonders of expression by just touching his/her partner’s hands.

- Don’t tell your partner what he/she should do. You are not the director and have to completely concentrate on yourself.
- Never say "NO" during an improv.

This means you can never refuse to accept the imaginary circumstances the other actor creates.
For instance, if you are asked: "What were you doing last night with Sylvia at the Opera?" you should never answer back, "You are wrong. I was not at the Opera last night" because you are literally killing the scene.

You have to choose a number of situations for your

improv although they might NOT BE part of the script.

Here is a list of improvs options:

- First encounter: How did they meet? Who took the initiative? Why did they want to see each other again?, etc.

- Was there a special moment when something very nice and unexpected happened? Did they overcome some difficult situation together?

- First time holding hands ... First kiss!

- First fight

- First really big fight.

- First reconciliation ... (Do choose one after the really big fight).

- The day he/she proposed ... (Yes, sometimes girls propose to guys.).

In the movie A MI ME GUSTA we could choose a number of scenes in Venezuela before Margarita leaves for England, then her interview and job relationship with Inga. We could also have some improvs about the deteriorating love affair between

Paul and Inga, Paul's professional dissatisfaction and lack of inspiration, etc.

For example if we are going to act the scene from the movie "STEPMOM" where Susan Sarandon is unable to tell Ed Harris she has cancer, it is advisable to do improvs on the first time they met, their first kiss, first big fight and subsequent reconciliation, the day he proposed to her, the day they decided to divorce, etc., etc.

The last improv will be ... improvising the very scene you have to play. It should start at the same point where the written scene begins. This way, you will have the opportunity to carefully watch yourself and ask two crucial questions:

- Would you react the way your character reacts in the play? ...

- Is there something you would do differently?

If your answer to the second question is yes, you might have to use better substitutions or be more logical and careful when you build up your character.

Physical actions: Please do find a physical action to perform during the scene, be it peeling an onion, putting tanning lotion on your arms, preparing and drinking a glass of whisky, polishing your nails, writing a letter, ... anything and everything.

A physical action can help you give a lot of information to the public in just a few seconds, so they understand the place where the character is and his sub-text. In real everyday life we are always doing several things at the same time. Only at the most decisive moments of the scene should our attention be completely focused on our acting partner.

Changes in the character's attitude do capture the audience's whole attention:

From silence to talking

From staring to moving

From action to freezing

The spectators need changes in order to be able to understand and share in the suspense of the scene. Every good scene has to bring about some change or new information. If it doesn't ...
it is probably useless.

Places have a strong influence on your acting. Every particular place will determine an important part of your behavior.
Acting in a McDonalds restaurant is very different from acting inside a church.

Sometimes you will be in a real scenario. If you are filming in the Venezuelan rain forest, you don´t have to worry: the heat and the mosquitoes will be there to help you, maybe even a multicolored snake drifting in the area.

More often, you will have to turn to the "theatre of your mind" for help.

What would you do if you had to play the tropical rain forest scene in a studio?

You have to ask yourself these questions:

To your mind, what place is similar for you to the location of the scene?

Is there a place you know that would trigger the same sensations the director is looking for?

Use Sense Memory with your eyes open to explore the place you remember ... Place yourself there and try to "touch" the objects that are supposed to be around you; smell and hear them.

We have to be aware that Sense Memory may be very personal and unpredictable. The impression that you have in a church might very well be the feeling other people experience in their bedroom.

Why wouldn't you try to visit a hospital, a Chinese restaurant, ... or your favorite bar so you can verify the power of each place and be aware of all the emotions you experience changing from one place to another?

Finally, clothing is a very important, too. It is different to dress like a Roman senator or soldier instead of an acting student. Different clothes will immediately modify your behavior. You might have to rehearse your scene several times in different clothes, then choose the attire that gets your best performance and suits you best.

NEXT STEP:

Start improvising your scene but use only four lines exactly as they are in the text: The very first one, the last one, and two somewhere in the middle.

Use your own words during the improv for the rest of your lines.

(Please realize that nothing is as noticeable -and annoying!- as an actor who STOPS HIS SCENE and gets lost trying to remember his lines. Even if you are on stage and this happens to you, JUST DON´T ... Put it in your words and charge ahead.)

After the improv, read your text flatly, without acting it, several times. It is most advisable that you use a recording device (journalist's recorder, MP3, etc) and tape the lines of your partner in the scene, leaving long enough blanks between them so you can say your lines during the silences.

You are ready now to meet the Director, who will give the final form to the scene according to his own artistic vision.

EMERGENCY KIT:

Sometimes, hopefully not too often, you will find unexpected difficulties in your work as an actor. You might not have enough time to study your character and lines properly; this often happens at soap operas, where you are handed your text just a few hours before filming. You can also go to a casting and be given the written scene a little while before you have to do your audition.

WHAT CAN I DO IN THIS CASE???

1. Learn your lines while taking out any emotions, objectives or intonations. Take just your lines and repeat them this way (do try to have an MP3!)

Do not pay attention to indications such as "strongly", "angry", "feeling deeply sad". These indications are there to explain the scene but you know by now that your sub-text is the real key.

2. Study the structure of the scene. There always is a change, ... maybe some important information. The scene would be meaningless otherwise.

Do discover the point of change, or the moment the new information comes up.

The dynamics of change is what makes a scene interesting to the public.

3. What is the most obvious form of acting the scene? Act it like that: obvious. Then throw it out once and for all and act it exactly the opposite way. After that, you will feel free to do whatever comes to your mind. Suppose you said your lines yelling out loud the first time ... Now say them calmly or laughing immediately afterwards.

4. As a rule of thumb, do not yell more than once in the same scene. One explosive reaction to a change or important new information will be more than enough.

5. NEVER, EVER ACT ANY SCENE ADDING A FEELING OF SELF PITY. The audience just hates such a character. You want sympathy, admiration, hatred, etc, from them. If the character is purposely sinking in his suffering and losing faith in having a solution to his problems, the spectators will refuse to have any empathy with him/her.

6. Crying doesn't equal good acting. Spectators will cry when a character experiences great pains and difficulties but doesn't lose faith in finding a solution

and keeps fighting. When a character breaks down but barely manages to avoid tears, it will be more interesting and will have more emotional value for the audience.

7. Text is of no value without silence.

Pauses make movement interesting.

There is no drama without smiles.

Opposites extremes give special meaning to a particular moment.

If you paint white on a white wall it will go unnoticed. A little black spot will catch the audience's undivided attention.

8. Take care of your partner. You don't have a scene without him/her.

9. Do not agonize if you have a day when you just don't want to act or feel completely uninspired. Go act and behave as naturally as you can. Every great actor/actress has a bad day every now and then but most people around them don't even notice.

Artists know it happens -"shit happens", Forrest Gump would say and don't feel guilty or confused.

Please remember we are playing, not saving lives nor performing neurosurgery.

There are rules, but all rules can be broken and have exceptions. Don't use Sense Memory when it is not necessary. If the character resembles you and you have a good intuitive grasp of him, just explore it from that point of view. You can always use Sense Memory later to solve some particular problem.

IF THERE ARE NO DIFFICULTIES, DON´T TRY TO SOLVE THEM

IF THERE IS NO PROBLEM, DON´T TRY TO CREATE ONE

The world is constantly changing. As an artist, you have to know it, learn to change, and look at yourself every day.

Know yourself. You can be intriguing, mysterious, exciting, dangerous, funny, daring, behave foolishly,... Then you can act characters who have these features. The limit is exactly the limit of your imagination.

Your biggest treasure is yourself, and your unique way of facing life. That is the reason why an actor like you will always be needed.

The Life of an Artist

INTRODUCTION

There are driving schools, cooking schools, schools to learn how to be a plumber. What about a college to learn how to be an artist?

We are not talking about how to learn your craft, be it painting, acting, or singing, but about a school where you explore what kind of life you live when you are an artist. Where to draw inspiration from, how to best motivate yourself, how to remain creative and constantly renewing your artistic vision.

First and foremost you have to understand that in this "production act", in this "job", ...

YOU MUST NEVER TAKE IT PERSONAL.

The content of your creation, your characters, your play, the message you want to convey as an artist, ... All these things are personal. But the production, the outside work, the way to take them to the audience, etc., are not personal.

There are people who have different plans from yours, and these persons will not help you to improve your artistic life. You need this professional attitude to help you not being stopped by small rocks you will find in your way.

Many people say "YOU JUST CAN’T". According to them, there are no new projects to be created, there is no work ...

It’s a permanent attitude of: "No, ... No, ... No ..." In my opinion, that is the voice of their own frustration, because if we can be sure of something it is precisely that all new creation is possible.
It is just plain good logic ! No “magic thinking”, no “wishing in the wind”, but understanding what it is artists do.

Let’s try to establish some rules that can be of help in this process:

1. Stick close to reality.

The point is not what your life should be like. The point is to start from your life basics - your real life as it is today, your social environment, your economic situation - and examine what is the new direction that your life is taking.

USE WHERE YOUR ARE AND STOP COMPLAINING!

(I have lived and worked in Europe, the US and South America and people COMPLAIN the exact same way everywhere and say: “if only I was born in….” all would be better)

2. You have to move in order to accomplish something.

It is not reasonable to just dream about being an actor / actress / artist then sit and wait for some producer to discover you. You have to physically get out of your home to try to get new opportunities and be your own “PRODUCER”.
The product? YOU.

3. The sheltering harbor.

In order to be creative in a permanent way, you need to be emotionally and financially secure. If you don’t know how you are going to pay the rent you just won’t have the peace of mind you need in order to work on that play you want to act. Of course, this doesn’t mean that you need to have millions in the bank; I am just saying that you need to have a feasible plan so that you’ll have a safe harbor.

PEOPLE DON’T PLAN TO FAIL, BUT FAIL TO PLAN!

Do notice that you don’t need to immediately change

your whole life in order to be an artist. Maybe becoming just a "part time" artist is a valid first step in the right direction.

4. The drama Queen/King.

Many people are convinced that you need to be poor, experience many difficulties, and lead a very "dramatic" life in order to be a real actor/ artist. This is quite wrong, a bad cliché. Like the Dalai Lama has said, life brings about enough drama and suffering and we don't need to add to it. On the other hand, nobody wants to work nor be with a "dramatic" person. Drama belongs up on the stage and not in your private and personal life. The most successful artists are serene and emotionally stable persons.

EMOTIONS

Most people make their decisions based on emotions. Now, if we carefully analyze the Sense Memory exercises we can observe that a thought or a word gives origin to emotion.

In order to be able to change the experience of your emotional body you need to change the way you focus on the object. In any given situation of your life, it is the mind that decides how you will feel about an event.

Some examples:

IMAGINE THAT YOUR BOYFRIEND/ GIRLFRIEND DUMPED YOU.

Option A. Great! You are closing an important cycle of your life and you have to allow yourself to feel the sadness of this event. Now, it is also true that you are giving yourself a chance to know a new partner. This means we can learn from broken relationships in order to make better choices and can take us to a new loving relationship.

Option B. Your self esteem is low, you enjoy suffering and imagine the worst: "THIS IS HORRIBLE! I won´t be able to have another boyfriend/girlfriend ever again" ... And you will feel that you have lost "LOVE" forever.

IMAGINE THAT YOUR CAR BROKE DOWN ...

Option A : Thank God it didn't happen during our trip to California!

Option B : DAMN LUCK! Life's not fair. Why do these things always happen to ME?

This is not only about being a positive and optimistic person, but about becoming aware that emotions are not useful to evaluate reality.

On the other hand, a toothache is a very different physical experience from our eventual emotional answer to it ("Why does it always happen to me? Why is my life full of suffering?")

If you pay closer attention to your emotional body you can manage to observe the roller coaster you have built inside you.

Rule: You are not your emotions. Don't confuse your emotions with your talent, instinct, or "inner voice"

FROM NOW ON, JUST OBSERVE HOW YOU GO THROUGH DIFFERENT EMOTIONAL STAGES DURING YOUR DAY.

The enthusiasm your projects awaken inside you and your perceptions about yourself and your work change constantly. In order to become a more productive artist you need to balance these elements.

Emotions such as euphoria and joyfulness are among the most pleasant ones. Now, let's consider for a moment that your completely open attitude to the "flow" of your emotions can be compared to an open dam in a strong river: you might not be able to "close" the gates when sadness and depression arrive. The river of your emotions will drag you on, time and again, from one extreme to the other, from euphoria to depression.

The only sensible option, then, will be to decide not to live at the extremes but to find emotional states that can be depicted as "peaceful" or "living the joy of each passing moment".
This choice is of the utmost relevance for the actor: Enjoying the present moment here and now and enjoying your work are also fundamental to a good acting performance.

THE MIND

Let's keep studying your instrument and focus on the way your mind works.

It very much resembles a computer. It is quite feasible to program it in order to produce positive thoughts even in difficult situations filled with obstacles.

Let's go back to the example of your broken down car:

If your mind is poorly prepared your first thought may be: "Why does it always happen to me?", triggering a series of chaotic and negative ideas that will make you lose a lot of time before you start looking for a solution.

YOUR ABILITY TO QUICKLY REACT TO UNEXPECTED EVENTS HAS A DIRECT INFLUENCE ON YOUR SUCCESS IN LIFE.

Practical example: The Director asks you to perform a new action in the movie. Your mind goes "Oh! I can't do that." As a result, the first take is a disaster.

"Action!" again and your mind goes to "Why didn't I prepare myself better? ... I AM PANICKING HERE !!!" After the 2nd take the Director is already thinking about firing you

All live shows call for actors to be able to improvise.

IF YOU GET STUCK IN THE MOMENT BEFORE, IF YOU GET STUCK IN YESTERDAY´S PROBLEM, ... YOU WON´T BE ABLE TO FIX THE PROBLEM YOU HAVE TO DEAL WITH **NOW**

Computers have a "trash can". And your mind has a trash can that keeps all the garbage you have thought and done during your whole life. That can, that archive in your mind, has to be emptied, so that it can function properly and make room for new data. Some forms of meditation are the only way to throw that garbage away.

In our society the word "meditation" has a religious connotation and many people don't do it just because they consider it to be a religious activity.

Let's rather call it "MENTAL HYGIENE, OR SYNCHRONIZING YOUR MIND" instead.

Stop all mental activity for 10 minutes.

Get away from all your thoughts of yesterday, thoughts of one hour ago, thoughts of five minutes ago, and just stay in the present.
Relax your emotional body, measuring this very moment for what it is, not for what it "should be " or "should not be".

When you can't sleep because you have an excess of thoughts and worries about tomorrow you need to clean your mind so that it doesn't behave like a computer that got stuck working on a sub-program and can't get out of the loop.

Counting sheep, the "proverbial" remedy people advise in order to fix your anguish, is just starting another program that will make your workload bigger and heavier.

It is quite feasible to train your mind and "think yourself" as you want to be.

Sense Memory and positive statements will do it for you.

The choice here is to guide your personal thoughts towards the creation of a better "personal world" instead of letting your mind do what your parents, teachers, and Society have already put inside you.

In order to reach a proper self-analysis we need to work on two important concepts: EGO and SELF ESTEEM.

Self-esteem, confidence in yourself, not needing to defend yourself from others nor needing to attack them, is essential for the good performance of any team.

The absence of self esteem (the EGO), destroys everything. EGO means that you are the only one having the right answers and the only one who has to be successful.
But if you are in a war against the rest of the world, the logical and inevitable outcome will be that nobody will want to help you.

WHEN THERE IS GOOD SELF ESTEEM THERE IS LITTLE EGO. AND VICE VERSA.

There are two ways of acquiring self-esteem in life.
The first is that your parents taught you from your early years to trust yourself and trust your own decisions.

If this didn’t happen you have a much more difficult task: As an adult, you have the power of stating your beliefs. You are not going to abide by any authority in your life who will explain to you how wonderful you are. Your mind will always object: "Who is this? ... How does he know?"

The point is that only you can help yourself, making yourself gifts because you have accomplished something. You need to consciously assert yourself and remind yourself of your successes every day.

Please check out the motivational videos on the www.miamiactingstudioblog.com in English and Spanish called “Acting Tips)

FEELINGS

"The memories, the past, the weight"

Frequently we remember our past decisions and think that now we would do things differently. We have a very bad opinion of our own experiences because we forget that everything is connected: our own art is connected to our life, our next project is developing within the possibilities of our entourage. To be an artist is a project in itself, and all the things happening around us are part of our lives and constitute the raw material our art is made of.

This thought leads us to realize that every artist has two possible ways of looking at life:

EVERYTHING IS CHAOS

THERE IS NO CHAOS

Many people have the conviction that there is an order in nature, in relationships among humans, and within physic laws. But they suddenly resort to explanations like "chance", "chaos", or "God" when events become chaotic, non linear, ...

IF YOU COULD ACCEPT THAT EVERYTHING IS CONNECTED AND THAT “THE UNIVERSE MAKES SENSE" ... WHAT WOULD HAPPEN TO YOUR VISION OF YOUR OWN LIFE?

If we apply this belief to feelings we may discover that they too have a reason for being, or that they have at least some useful purpose for us.

It all began when Homo Sapiens lived in caves and everything outside was dreadful, anything new or stressful was dangerous. The army of his subconscious would always try to protect him from the unknown because that is where the deadly dangers were hiding.

Growth, movement, and even success are stressful changes.

Our subconscious doesn’t know the difference between a "change for the better" and "change that brings suffering".
It is only about PREVENTING CHANGE.

If our subconscious mind could talk, it would say something like this when you walk out of an important casting:

"If I’m lucky ... If I get the main part ... I have to move from my mother’s house to a place closer to TV studio because I can’t drive three hours a day. I’ll have to share an apartment with other people so the rent doesn’t become too expensive. All this will cause many conflicting situations as my boyfriend/girlfriend is really jealous as it is..

Hey, these other people could steal my things at the apartment.

....And even if it all goes OK, I will have to move to California to because that’s what actors do.... BUT I don’t know anybody there! I will be soooo lonely.....

"NO, NO, NO ... ", our subconscious yells ... And it so happens that you don’t feel comfortable with yourself the very day you have an important casting audition.

Or all of a sudden you “FEEL” that this project "is not worth it" and then you decide it is much better to wait for a better moment.

Please pay attention to the relationship between the "stress level" caused by the new opportunity and the size of the stones that you put on your own path in order not to get the new job.

THE ONLY OPTION HERE IS TO OBSERVE THE

GAMES PLAYED BY THE SENTIMENTAL INNER WORLD, THEN GET FAMILIAR WITH THE STRESS GENERATED BY OUR SUCCESS AND MANAGE TO EXPAND OUR LIFE SCOPE.

Remember not to make it personal (your ART is personal, but NOT the business part of it) in order to avoid getting stuck to feelings of guilt. This is a work of art in progress, and you want to have everything coming out right, but you have to be patient.

Now, how do I do not to take it personal if this is so important to me?

Actors would save themselves a lot of frustration if they could get better information about artistic and professional processes, getting to know how a play or a TV series are planned and produced. They often prefer to believe that the MAGIC of CASTING will make them a big star overnight. This belief gets them wielding all power and responsibility for their own artistic lives to other people.

Let's examine a few specific cases where our professional life seems to be particularly unfair:

Question: Since I am right and have a better way to solve the problem, why doesn't the Director listen to me?

Answer: Because he is the Director, period. He has his own vision and ... if things come out bad his head is on the line.

Question: Why doesn't the Director help me more? How come he/she doesn't tell me how to perform better? Why doesn't he spend more time with me?

Answers: He has to worry about a lot of things (camera, producers, time, rating, etc). Not only about the actors.

As an actor, you have to prepare several ways of acting the scene. He is the one to choose among them.

The Director is neither your best friend nor your mortal enemy. He doesn't have a personal agenda with you (although many actors and actresses are convinced of the contrary, sadly enough).

Question: Why don't they give me the main part, the lead?

Answers: Think public relations. You need to develop a good marketing strategy. What can you do better than anyone else?
Maybe you simply are not what the Director has in mind for the part. Even if you are a fabulous actor, aren't they looking for an older one, maybe?

Even if you are really great, maybe you look haggard, stressed out, strange ... and the Director prefers someone with a more stable and reliable "feel".

When you entered the audition premises your lack of self esteem was noticeable. Maybe you were talking too much, ... or you stayed silently sitting on a chair like a scared kid. The casting Director is aware of everything you do from the very moment you arrive and thus your lack of preparation kept you from showing your real talent.

THE BODY

"I am sleepy" ... "I don't feel like it" ... I'm tired" ... These are sentences we use to express some physical distress and we should pay more attention to it. Our physical body is our vehicle and we need it to function properly on our path to success.

Stress and emotional lack of balance complicate the "chemical cocktail" in your veins, literally. As a matter of fact, every thought and every emotion do generate neuro-chemicals and neuro-peptids that circulate in our bodies.

Quite often, and somewhat paradoxically, it is only when we make progress in our artistic work that we come to realize the damage stress can inflict on us in the form of psychosomatic illnesses. For example: One actress did an excellent job during the filming of the movie A MI ME GUSTA but then, right after the movie was finished she would stay in bed all day, stopped going to the gym, etc. If success can be stressful, low creativity, artistic rejection, drastic changes from one project to another, etc., is even worse.

You do not have to wait to start taking care of your health.

YOU NEED A PHYSICAL EXERCISE PROGRAM THAT WILL HELP YOU ELIMINATE THE EFFECTS OF STRESS. CHECK YOUR PHYSICAL CONDITION REGULARLY.

MONEY

If you are just starting your artistic career it is not likely that you will be earning enough money next week to cover all your expenses.

You have to make a budget, planning based on reality and ... not on wishful thinking.

First of all, make a list of all of your monthly expenses.

This is a rather painful exercise since you will be criticizing yourself for every dollar you spend, but it is very valuable in order to know real data and to decide how much you can invest in your "artistic happiness" ... Yes, you always have to set aside a small weekly amount to make yourself little gifts that will motivate you and increase your productivity.

Your relationship to money is obviously very important and there is an interesting exercise to "get used" to having it :

Put on the side 10% of what you earn in a secret place, cash. This 10% is to be used only on a future

investment such as a piece of real estate or a serious emergency.
Get used to looking at this box with cash inside every time you are worried about money, so that you can give yourself a feeling of security. To make this moment dramatic and amusing say out loud "YES, I CAN!" when you watch it, thus enjoying your discipline and perseverance.

As you can see, this is not about playing THE AVARE by Molière, nor imitating the character SCROOGE by Dickens.

THE MATRIX

I want to share a few more thoughts with you before we get to the exercises: Your awareness of prosperity, your subconscious mind, and your self-esteem do build up your environment.

Everything around you is a mirror reflecting the way you look at life, your way of adding value to it.

An old Chinese proverb says: "Luck doesn't exist. It is just an event that meets with an prepared mind". Our success and our rapid artistic growth depend on ourselves and our ability to continue to create.

Have you known people who are always suffering? ... People who are always unlucky? ... who have relationships that never work? ... who have boyfriends/girlfriends who leave them? ... People who lose all their money and go bankrupt?

These people get stuck in the thought that "life is not fair" and spend most of their energy trying to explain to you why things are not possible, WHY PROJECTS CAN'T BE ACCOMPLISHED. Their fear is too big. Their ego and lack of self-esteem don't allow them to look for help.

Imagine a little "RESET" button to "re-boot" your system as if it was for the first time. What if you would look at your world today for the first time? Your life, your job, your work, your life plan ? It would open the door to:

A. Solutions based on reality (not on daydreams).

B. Never giving up.

C. Not taking things personally.

From that moment on, everything becomes "the next lesson" or the revisiting of a chapter already lived. It can also become the next play you are going to write.

Nowadays we accept the notion that every action calls for a reaction and that there is no way that energy can disappear; it just transforms itself.

We also know that our thoughts are made of small electric waves that will have an effect around us: they will not vanish but will show up later in a different, energetically useful state.

Whether you want to call this process Synchronicity, as the great German psychologist C.G.Jung did, or if you prefer to call it "magic", or just "taking advantage of artistic life", the key is to get out of your mind and DO things (study, work, research, ask, etc.). Art is born from sharing. The inspiration is outside you. You have to look for it and start imagining.

EXERCISES

1. WRITE

We artists experience a certain creative loneliness. Our talent is private, very intimate, as is our connection with it. We will include here some exercises meant to help your artistic growth. Each person has his own rhythm in this self-exploration and only you can decide how much time you want to invest in this process.

In order for your creativity to take shape and become real you have to manage to bring your ideas to written form and put your fantasy and imaginative life into a text that can be used as a reference next time you take back to your project. Here is an exercise to help create this connection: It also functions as a "mental hygiene tool" and its name is "MY INVENTORY"

For the next **THREE MONTHS**, write three pages every morning. This is not a diary, nor is it your autobiography, but simply the act of recording what is going on in your mind, literally, in order to know all your thoughts no matter how chaotic or confused they may be. You don't dwell on them or feel guilty about your frustrations.

When you are sleeping, your mind changes "frequency" and enters the world of dreams and nightmares. It is only proper that you stimulate your mind in the morning so you can get it in contact with reality and think clearly. It is a “stream of consciousness”.

Here is an example of what it might look like:

"I am horribly sleepy, I truly hate Mondays. Oh, last night’s party was great. To work. Difficult. Sleepy. I can’t stand Jack, it’s not that I hate him, he just annoys me. Don’t want to go to that damned meeting. See, that is the problem. I don’t want to work. I have to stop having heavy food for dinner, it gives me nightmares. Why didn’t I start working on my acting earlier, like years ago. I really want to ACT, don’t want to go to more castings... "

As you can see, there is no logic or cohesiveness. Your mission at this point is just to get to the end of your three pages and empty the trashcan of your mind. You’ll always have important glimpses about what you want to do and what you don’t want to do, things you love and things you hate. Sometimes you can spend days complaining without finding any answer. The only simple rule to follow in order to overcome these unproductive days is ... to keep on writing these three pages every single day without missing a single one.

After writing these pages, just throw them away without reading them. If your work schedule makes it really impossible for you to write in the morning, choose a more convenient time but never stop working on this aspect of your artistic life. Now that you have an everyday connection to your talent you may choose three particular moments during your working day in order to check and nurture your **SYSTEM**. You can choose these control points as you like, for instance at 11 am, 3 pm and 5 pm. Set your alarm.

Get used to inhaling deeply, noticing how you feel and what you need. When you begin to actively take care of your talent on a daily basis, your quality of life will improve and your creativity will be enhanced.

2. MAKE STATEMENTS

As previously said, our mind can be compared to a computer storing information. Sadly enough, a lot of negative statements have been stored in our hard drive: sentences like, "All artists are poor", "I'm nothing special", "I'll never be better", to name but a few. Many of these sentences (mental laws) are not there as result of a learning process or personal discovery of ours, but because we "always" heard them, although they do not reflect our reality.

These statements were "lodged" there by your teachers and family members in order to protect you and guide you during your growth period. Unfortunatly, your brain can't tell the difference between a "useful sentence" and an "old sentence".

A stressful situation will trigger these thoughts without giving you a chance to control them.

You need to prepare your mind for this eventuality. Sooner or later it will happen, and you will need to have a positive mental attitude. Here is a list of statements as a guide to help you find your own personal ones:

I .... love myself, and fully and affectionately approve of myself.

I ....do connect myself with the joy of being alive.

I .... love life.

When I ....was born the universe rejoiced in it and filled me with love, health and prosperity.

For me ....the source of love and prosperity flows freely in my body.

I ....remain open to receiving everything the universe offers me.

I ....deserve happiness in my everyday life.

I ....trust my talents and myself.

I ....trust my artistic and spiritual growing process.

I ....connect myself with the energy of God inside me.

I ....acknowledge and accept the power of God inside me.

Choose one of these statements every day and write it 11 times on a sheet of paper, filling the blanks with your own name.

For example: ***"I, Ralph, acknowledge and accept the power of God in my life"***

Then, write on the same piece of paper your doubts about it. For example: ***"I, Ralph, accept the power of god inside me ... Ah!, What about God, I don't believe any of it, it's corny, God didn't help me last Thursday, why does he make everything so damned difficult ... "***

Don't finish until you feel you have expressed all your feelings about the subject.

After having worked for one month with this list, create your own list of statements.

Next, write on the left side of a sheet of paper all the problems that you see in your life. Then, on the right side you'll write the positive version of that sentence.

Example:

I never finish my projects ***I always finish my projects***

I feel poor I'm prosperous

I'm always sick I'm healthy

I feel I am a failure I'm a total success

I have no talent I am a talented person

Finally, make a statement that combines the five most important elements.

Example:

I am a prosperous, successful, healthy and loved person who always finishes his projects.

YOUR STATEMENTS MUST INCLUDE ONLY THE VERBS "TO BE" AND "TO DESERVE". IF YOU USE THE VERBS "TO WANT" OR "TO WISH" YOU WILL CAUSE FRUSTRATION AND FEELINGS OF GUILT FOR NOT HAVING ACCOMPLISHED YOUR GOAL YET.

You can adapt these sentences to new situations in your life. Your mind is guided by what you have established as your basic reality, and this is how it selects the information it allows to come in. Be aware how your mind works here:

If I ask you right now to get connected to your right foot, you immediately know how it feels. If I don't ask, you don't pay attention to it and you let any information about your foot go unnoticed. Since there is so much information reaching you all the time, your mind rejects much new data without you even being aware of this process, in order to avoid a surcharge.

For instance, if you want to buy new shoes, you will acquire the reflex of looking at people's shoes around you.

If you think you will never have enough money, you'll always get jobs you'll never be satisfied with.

If you think relationships never work, you will only find unstable people.

If you think directors want to take advantage of you, you will attract unprofessional people.

If you think life is ugly and unfair, your mind will work overtime to prove that opinion.

Since it is easier to observe this bad dynamic in other people than acknowledge it in ourselves, ask yourself if you know a friend or member of your family who spends his whole life penniless (even if he/she works), complaining about everything, always stressed, frustrated and unhappy about his/her personal relationships. This kind of person may change jobs or friends but will keep repeating the same mental patterns and will end up having the same bad life situations.

Remember that a statement is not a magic tool or a portrait of your immediate reality, but a description of your creative potential. Even when you are using these sentences, you have to knock on all possible doors. When you make the attempt and enter these new doors you will realize the positive effect of your previous inner work.

3. GET ENERGIZED

When I hear people talking about **ENERGY** I immediately imagine a blue energy "ball" from a Japanese animated movie and the good guys beating the hell out of the bad guys. Then, of course, the possibility of using a magic ball in my everyday life is very close to zero.

But you have probably noticed that:

Some conversations just leave me exhausted while others motivate me and get me smiling at once.

Some working days just fly by while others are long and tough.

Sometimes I get a phone call that makes me happy and awakens my will to create.

Sometimes I party all night long and the next day I wake up early wanting to party again, while other parties make me tired and I get up in the morning feeling horrible.

Sometimes my back and shoulders ache because I had a bad night's sleep.

Sometimes I get up in the morning after a more

than eight hours rest but I am still sleepy.

Some thoughts make me feel sad, confused.

Worrying about the future makes me feel heavy.

Watching TV for hours makes me feel out of order and filled with chaos.

Let's have a closer look at these "energies". We are all connected at a given level of energy and certain people around us can have such a negative influence that they take the motivation out of us, even when they don't say anything!

Self-motivation, getting up every morning with the will and stamina to **"conquer the world"** requires a lot of work. That is precisely the reason why you have to take appropriate measures to maintain your creativity and to protect your inner artist.

There are two kind of people around you: one kind supports you and the other drags you down. Your biological family (parents, siblings, children, etc.) are people who have a very precise vision of what you should be doing in life.

SINCE THESE ARE EMOTIONAL RELATIONSHIPS, THESE PEOPLE NEED YOU TO HAVE A CERTAIN BEHAVIOUR SO

THAT THEIR WORLD DOESN´T EXPERIENCE CHANGES.

The fact that you want to change doesn't mean the people around you are going to understand and grow with you. Sharing genes doesn't mean they HAVE to share your dreams.

Anyone who says anything like **"Good, but I didn't understand it", "Excellent, but it can't be made"** without giving you a better way of doing it is actually performing an attack on your artistic life and drawing strength out of your dream.

Sentences from your friends and family like **"I didn't express it well", "It's for your own good", "I just want the best for you"** can be very treacherous because they tend to make you have confidence in someone who is not helping you at all.

You are not "bad" because you have secrets, but since artistic dreams tend to be vague, people get scared when they hear their son or best friend talking about a creative adventure.

Your **artistic family** is made up of people you meet in your life who are like you; people who know to listen to you without imposing their preconceived ideas or criticizing you; people who are willing to support you and keep you motivated and cheerful. It is extremely difficult to formulate a constructive critical opinion on a given creative project. It can only be considered truly "constructive" if that opinion gives an alternate way of realization that is more feasible, more convenient.

This also means we have to be very careful about what advice we give to others, since we can only judge things from your own experience.

Let's do an exercise now: Draw a circle on a blank sheet of paper and inside write the names of all the people belonging to your artistic family.
Outside the circle write the names of the people who are not supportive. You don't have to feel guilty about the latter: in most cases they don't mean to hurt you.

Draw one more circle on another paper and inside it write all your ideas and goals that need protecting. Outside of the circles all the ideas you can share without danger. Remember to take care of the ideas INSIDE the circle: they need to be taken care of, for they are your dearest and most intimate artistic dreams.

You have a "self-defense" mechanism that can slow down your success:
Personal growth brings about personal changes. Your

body and your subconscious tend to consider changes as potential dangers. As a result, they resist and oppose the idea of initiating something new.

When you are aware of this you can help yourself not to fall into your own traps. Since we all the ways and means of sabotaging ourselves, try this following exercise:

1. Make a list of five types of fights you frequently have.

2. Name five things that make you feel tired.

3. List five things you like about yourself.

4. Make a list of five things you have accomplished in life.

5. Make a list of five people who helped you to believe in yourself as an artist.

6. Among your many thoughts, which are the ones that make you scared about being an artist?

7. Are you a perfectionist? ("There are no mistakes. We are all a work in progress".)

Your perfectionism is an obstacle to your growth.

8. Have you suddenly lost interest in a project, without a clear and specific reason?

9. Did you lose interest, right after making some progress or accomplishing something?

10. Have you noticed that inexplicably, like magic, you never manage to "find the time" to work on your project?

11. Have you become obsessive about things like:

Eating too much, sleeping too much, complaining too much, not sleeping enough, wasting time in waiting lines, watching too much TV, taking drugs, working too much, calling your most destructive friends, spending too much time in the gym ...?

12. Do you happen to know someone willing to help you, but you discarded this person because it was just "too good to be true"?

13. On the contrary, do you feel that another person should help you, take over your projects or your search in life, so that you only have to wait?

14. Have you brought drama to your personal life, instead of bringing it to your artistic life?

15. Are you in a permanent fight with your

sweetheart?

16. Have you given priority to your relatives´ interests over yours? Do you think the problems of friends of yours who seem to always be in a state of "emotional crisis" are more important than your problems?

17. Do you spend a lot of your time with people who always have the same problems with their sweethearts, with money, alcohol, depression, etc.?

18. Are you losing your time trying to "save" everybody?

19. Which of your relatives advise you not to get into producing art?

20. Who is using up your energy?

21. Which people have the knowledge and experience to help you make progress?

22. Fear will always be there. What are the specific fears that your project triggers inside you?:

23. Being successful stresses me out because ....

24. I am scared of producing art because ....

25. I am ashamed or scared of asking for help because ....

THERE ARE NO MISTAKES. THERE ARE JUST LEARNING OPPORTUNITIES.

Imagine that your fear is an entity that will use any possible means in order to keep you from changing. This entity (this person if you prefer to picture it this way) has a number of weapons to use against you: SHAME, GUILT, HATRED, AND DEPRESSION.

Let's consider a few examples that can illustrate the subtle dynamics of fear:

*** You are suddenly "ashamed" to ask advice from the father of your best friend, although you know that he works in a media you would like to get familiar with.**

*** To study acting makes you spend less time with your boyfriend/girlfriend and you feel guilty about it.**

*** You are in your first acting lesson and you suddenly feel that you know nothing and you'll never be any good at it (although many of the other students have the same fear).**

*** An actress knows a casting director who wants to have her pictures and maybe call her for an audition. She assumes he won't like her pictures and never calls him.**

*** A well known writer wants to read the play of an amateur writer in order to help him. The new writer never shows his play because he assumes it's not worth it.**

Sometimes, just after we have overcome a big difficulty, we start doubting our recently proven success and start to be late, stop getting prepared every day, start fighting and creating conflict, etc.

These fears do exist. Shame exists. Wish of sabotaging ourselves is often there. But our goal has to be "marching on" in spite of all those negative feelings, not allowing them to destroy our well deserved success.

4. EMERGENCY LIST

If you feel bad today, are not motivated, or just feel "out of order", please hang on to this ARTISTIC EMERGENCY LIST:

1. What happened during the last three days. What made you feel this way?

2. There is nothing you can do to avoid those feelings. You already have them!

3. Remember the last time you felt that way and remember that life went on afterwards.

4. Call an artist friend and invite him/her to have a cup of coffee right away.

5. Schedule your day properly, like in any other job:

8 - 9 buy food
9 - 10 breakfast and reading e mails, etc.

6. Do not stay home on days like this.

7. Get support. Send an email with your name to news@miamiactingstudio.com and receive every week free motivational and sign up for a free consultation with me over the phone, skype, email or

in person at consultation@miamiactingstudio.com.

8. Take a day to try and get a small but authentic smile.

5. GET SYNCHRONIZED

Artistic life, like any other job, demands some amount of discipline that gives shape to your daily work. Your artist needs to "dress up" his mind in the morning; this means getting ready for a creative work's day. Let's call this activity "synchronizing the mind". Let's compare this activity to tuning on your radio in order to have better reception and knowing "what is today's program?"

Stop reading for moment and watch the sheet of paper you are reading.

Turn it upside down.

Smell it.

What do you feel? (do **not** answer)

Now, look around you.

What time is it?

What can you hear?

During the 10 seconds you were doing this exercise, without realizing it you were "synchronizing your mind", "meditating" about the moment. You started to tie yourself to the present.

In order to create the world that you want, repeat this exercise at least twice a day, increasing little by little the time you devote to it until you reach 10 minutes. You will learn to have more and more moments of clarity.

You probably experienced that your emotions calmed down during those 10 seconds and you forgot your worries for a moment.

The most amazing thing about artistic research is that **the happier you are, the more creative and successful you become.**

When you manage to find the "will to fight" in life, your creativity will give you wings to make you able to overcome any obstacle.

6. FORGIVENESS DIET

But ... What can I do if the memories of the past and all the things that I "supposedly" did wrong keep me from seeing the new horizon?

What can I do if I don´t give myself freedom to enjoy myself with art, and I can only feel guilt?

What do I do when my mind keeps telling me I´m losing my time living an aimless life that makes me bitter and robs me of the possibility of trying new things?

The next exercise, called "The Forgiveness Diet", was created to free you from this tension. To judge our present by the rules of the past will shut the door to the limitless new opportunities that pop up at every moment. You are going to forgive yourself, and you are going to forgive other people, so you can leave the past behind you. This exercise consists of writing forgiveness letters. Send the first letter to yourself, in this form:

"I .... forgive myself completely and lovingly for ...." (write all the things that make you feel guilty here)

Example:

I, Ralph, forgive myself completely and lovingly for not being chosen at the casting for the AT&T commercial, for performing badly, for being scared of calling Steve Soderbergh, for putting too much pressure on myself, for breaking plates in my house when I was 8 and having fights with my sister about money, etc, etc.

You will see that many times we feel very bad about things that seem meaningless to others but crucial for us because we are sensible artists. These little pains take confidence and strength away from us on our way forward.

When you feel that you have written everything that comes to your mind today, put this piece of paper away and NEVER READ IT !

DESTROY IT IMMEDIATELY

Do exactly the same thing the next day. Repeat the same conflicts and add new ones that come to your mind. Do it for seven consecutive days.

On week number two you are going to forgive your mother.

On week number three you are going to forgive your

father.

The 4th week will be dedicated to your sweetheart, life partner etc., and the 5th will be dedicated to other people ...

Finally, you are going to forgive God. It may seem amazing that you have to forgive God, but there are events that are "nobody´s fault" and must be placed on that most particular list, such as:

... allowing hunger to be widespread in the world, making things so difficult in life, ...

BEAUTY IS AN AGREEMENT BETWEEN CONTENT AND FORM

(Henrik Ibsen)

7.PLAY

After so much self-exploration and discipline, we finally arrive to the most amusing game, "Play date".

In the end, it is fun that leads us to creativity, but as adults we are so stressed out, we need a map that will make us have fun.

Imagine for a moment a beautiful garden full of trees with fruits on them (apples, oranges, cherries, ...) as a representation of our ideas.

If you pick fruits every day but don't take care of the garden, ... the fruits will be finished.

You ruined your garden because you didn't worry about the ecological system: Trees need to be watered, sun shields are necessary in some places, weeds have to be removed, etc.

Your artistic garden needs caring too. You have to refill your inspiration in order to maintain your ecological system.

This date with your artist takes place once a week, when you spend a fixed amount on something funny.

The rules are:

*** You have to spend time alone, without your sweetheart, friends or family.**

***You have to go out of your house.**

***You are not permitted to do anything "intellectual", like going to a museum if that bores you. You have to entertain your artist.**

Some examples are: Have a good ice cream, visit a video game store, pretend you are going to buy a Harley-Davidson, buy an exotic CD, buy flowers for your home, buy paint, rent a bike, ...

The most useful part about finding out what your 10 favorite things to get your spirit up is, that it will help you raise your spirits the day you feel empty, defeated, disappointed ... And you will do it without anybody's help.

Do plan something different every week, be it an urban adventure or a little unexpected surprise, so your life is filled with many colors, tastes, and refreshing experiences.

8.DREAM

"Your dreams and longings come from God ("universal power")".

He (it) has the power of making your dreams come true. Dreaming would make no sense otherwise.

Everything can be accomplished. It just takes the right strategy to make it happen.

If you are experiencing difficulties and are looking for "inspiration" to move forward, here is an interesting exercise:

Pay attention to your nightly dreams.

Place a notebook next to your bed and when you wake up write what you dreamt.

If you are looking for a solution to a specific problem, write on your notebook something like this:

Dear innerself,

Please reveal to me in a dream five images that will help me understand and solve the problems I have with the character Tom Broker in the movie "The Lord of the Horses".

With love and respect.

Signed: Your name.

It is quite probable that within the next five days you have a dream that might inspire you. Observe that dream as something funny, or as a beautiful secret that is inside you.

9. DISCOVER

Success is directly related to your ability to let yourself be loved. The best gift life can give you is that the audience considers you to be so important that you get their undivided attention.

If they do but then this emotion causes you anguish and stress, your subconscious mind will do anything to protect you and draw you apart from the situation.

A team better solves all the difficulties you are finding in your path.

Art is teamwork. You have to know when to look for help and stop wasting your energy and motivation without making progress by trying to fix everything by yourself

Who can give you advice?

Remember that we humans are all different. That is the reason why there is a place for each one of us. We have to look for that individuality inside each of us, and celebrate it.

Your work as an artist is to pay attention to your talent: it will guide you about what is the best way of showing what you know. Life is so great that there is no way to "trap" it. Our mission is to live it and say yes to all the opportunities that appear on your way.

Our work is to look for the renewal of the mind, the “beginner’s mind”.

To watch the sun rise as if were the first one you experienced at this place and in this body.

To renew the decision every day to live always remembering how incredible it is that right now there is air going in and out of your body.

And above anything else, just work on being happy.

ABOUT THE AUTHOR:

Ralph Kinnard has been teaching for over ten years acting and directing to hundreds of actors, directors, models, TV and Radio hosts. He is a successful, award winning director and his unique approach to teaching emotional intelligence and intuitive intelligence have made him a sought after keynote speaker for international companies such as Bayer, Deutsche Bank, Banco Central Universal, Kraft, Mastercard and others...

For more information visit : www.miamiactingstudio.com

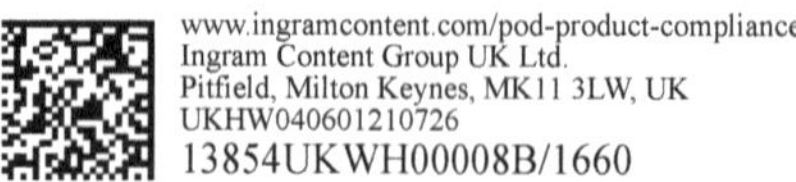
www.ingramcontent.com/pod-product-compliance
Ingram Content Group UK Ltd.
Pitfield, Milton Keynes, MK11 3LW, UK
UKHW040601210726
13854UKWH00008B/1660

9 781105 555442